*mine*dition

North American edition published 2015 by Michael Neugebauer Publishing Ltd. Hong Kong

Text copyright © 2011 Géraldine Elschner

Translated by Kathryn Bishop, English text adaptation by Martin West

Picture segments from Frescos in the chapel Scrovegni (Padova) by Giotto die Bondone (1266 - 1337)

Michael Neugebauer Publishing Ltd., Unit 23, 7/F, Kowloon Bay Industrial Centre,

15 Wang Hoi Road, Kowloon Bay, Hong Kong. Phone +852 2807 1711, e-mail: info@minedition.com

This book was printed in May 2015 at L.Rex Printing Co Ltd 3/F., Blue Box Factory

Building, 25 Hing Wo Street, Tin Wan, Aberdeen, Hong Kong, China

Typesetting in Silentium Pro designed by Jovica Veljovic

Library of Congress Cataloging-in-Publication Data available upon request.

ISBN 978-988-8240-46-3

10 9 8 7 6 5 4 3 2 1

First Impression

For more information please visit our website: www.minedition.com

THE NATIVITY

Retold by Géraldine Elschner
with Pictures by Giotto
translated by Kathryn Bishop

minedition

One morning in the spring,
a voice sounded in Mary's house.

"Fear not,"
said the angel Gabriel.
"God has chosen you.
You shall bear a son and shall name him Jesus.
He shall be called the Son of God."

Mary was astonished and knelt down saying,
"Let it be done as you have said."

Once she knew of the child,
she began to love him.
She loved with her whole heart,
and without hesitation.

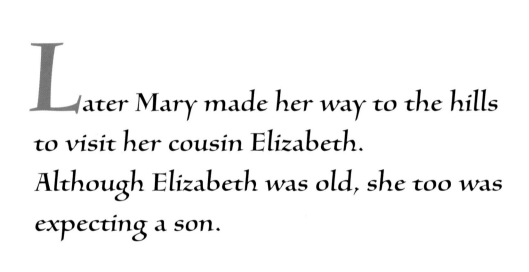

*L*ater Mary made her way to the hills
to visit her cousin Elizabeth.
Although Elizabeth was old, she too was
expecting a son.

When Mary greeted her, Elizabeth felt
the child move in her womb.
He was to be called John,
and would become John the Baptist.

In time, Mary returned home.
In her house in Nazareth,
her long wait would be beautiful and calm,
beside Joseph, whom she had taken
as her husband.

As the child grew within her, a decree
was sent out from Caesar Augustus.
Every resident should be counted in
the city of his birth.
As a son of the house of David, Joseph
had to return to Bethlehem in Judea,
where he was born.
And so he and Mary set out on their way.

The journey was long through the icy winds of winter.
The little donkey that carried Mary made slow progress.
Under her cloak, the young mother protected the child within her as best she could.
It would soon be time for the child to come into the world.

When they finally arrived in Bethlehem, the city was crowded with travelers.
They too had come to be counted.

But there was no room in the inn.
No roof. No bed for Mary.

In an old stable they found rest for the night.
And on a bed of straw Mary gave birth to her son.

There were shepherds in the fields watching their flocks.
And while they were resting, the sky was suddenly bright.

The men were terrified.
"Fear not," said an angel. "I bring you good tidings of great joy.
A savior is born.
Peace on Earth!
You will find the child
wrapped in swaddling clothes,
lying in a manger."

"A child?
A savior?
Nearby, in a stable?"

Curious, the men hurried under the starry sky,
to Bethlehem, to search for the baby.

They found him in a manger,
sheltered between the ox and donkey.
And they brought baskets with
furs, wool and milk.

Quietly the sheep lay down.

Far, far away from Bethlehem,
wise men in the East saw a strange
star in the heavens.

And they followed it,
through mountains and valleys,
through forests and deserts.
The star led them to the stable,
where they found the child with
his mother.
They knelt down before him to offer
their treasures of gold, frankincense
and myrrh.

Mary watched everything around her.
These were sights and sounds she would
never forget.
She kept them in her heart, and throughout
her life, she would remember.

Soon, she thought, we will return home.
Soon we will again find our house, our village
and our family.

After the wise men from the East had left,
Joseph had a dream ...
"Get up," said an angel. "You must take the
child and his mother and flee to Egypt. Herod
is searching for him and intends to kill him."

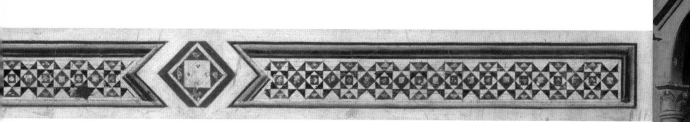

Herod! King Herod.
News had also spread to him of the birth
of the new king.
The Prince of Peace.
Anger and jealousy filled Herod's heart.
He alone should wear the crown!
So he sent his soldiers to find all those
who were newly born.

His wrath was boundless.
Mary's child was in danger.
They had to flee!

That same night, Joseph rose,
determined to bring mother and child
to safety.

Mary sighed.
The journey would be long.

Again Joseph led them.
And again the little donkey, loyal and loving,
carried Mary over grass and stone.

This time, however, she carried her child in
her arms.
Here he was warm.
Here there was milk.
Here he was secure, protected from the world.
And she would always be with her son …

A lways,
until the end.

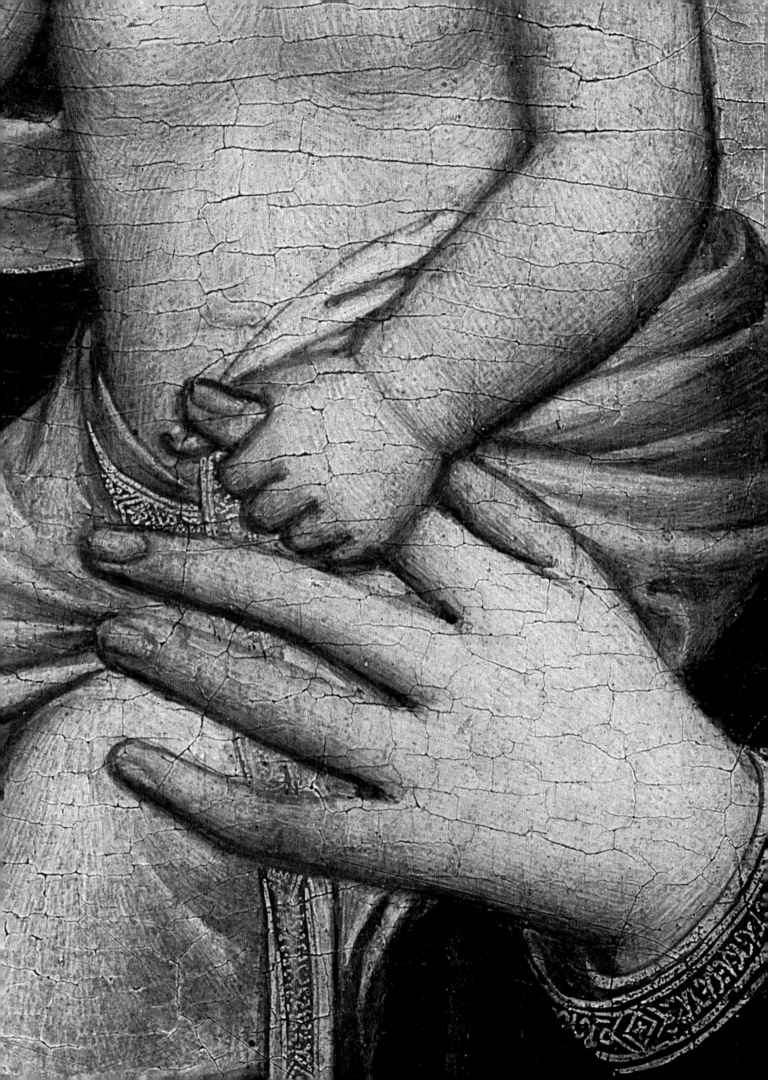